Wham! Undersea

A Killer Food Chain

by

Sean Callery

Illustrated by Shona Grant

With special thanks to our reader:
Daniel Hall

First published in 2009 in Great Britain by
Barrington Stoke Ltd
18 Walker St, Edinburgh, EH3 7LP

www.barringtonstoke.co.uk

Title ISBN: 978-1-84299-712-3
Pack ISBN: 978-1-84299-786-4

Printed in Great Britain by The Charlesworth Group

Intro

About 70 per cent of the Earth is covered by water.

Sea water is salty, not like the fresh water of rivers and lakes.

Salt water between continents is bigger than the sea and is called an ocean.

The sea can be so deep that it would cover the highest mountains in the world if they were resting on the seabed.

Sea food

Every living thing is part of a food chain. Everything has to eat to stay alive. There are many food chains in the sea and most sea creatures are part of more than one chain.

Life can be hard in the sea. Everything has to eat to stay alive, and if you are not careful, you can be an animal's next meal.

Wham! Goodbye Sun, hello sea plant

Sea plants grow up at the Sun's rays and use its light to make their food.

Wham! Goodbye sea plant, hello plankton

Many billions of tiny creatures called 'plankton' live in the sea.

They are smaller than a full stop. These 'plankton' can't swim – they just drift about.

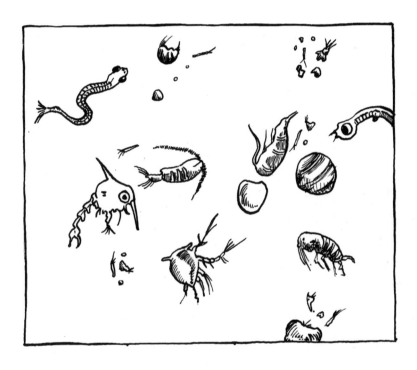

Wham! Goodbye plankton, hello shrimp

Shrimps live on the bottom of the sea. They don't have fins like fish but they can still swim by jerking their bodies.

They eat plankton.

Could it kill me?

No, but shrimps that have not been well cooked and still have germs in them can give you a very nasty tummy bug if you eat them.

Yuk!

Wham! Goodbye shrimp, hello jelly fish

Jelly fish have no bones, eyes or brains.

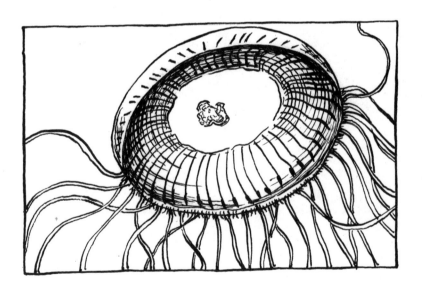

They are just blobs with long arms
called tentacles.

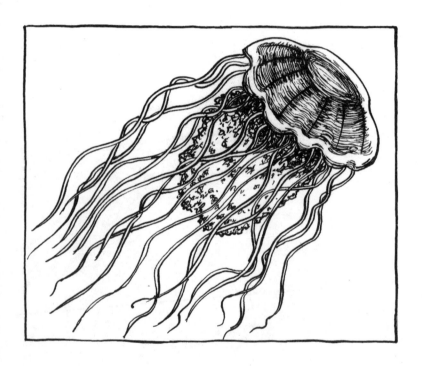

Each of these tentacles has a sting to catch prey. The jelly fish stuns its prey then pulls it into its mouth.

Jelly fish eat shrimps.

Could it kill me?

Some jelly fish stings are strong enough to kill a human. Even a small sting can hurt a lot. If you get stung many times you could drown from the pain and shock.

Wham! Goodbye jelly fish, hello tuna

Tuna can grow as big as a man. They swim very fast and have many sharp teeth to catch their prey.

They eat smaller fish and jelly fish.

Could it kill me?

No, but people are killing them off. We eat so much tuna that there are less and less of them in the sea – which means there are more jelly fish.

Wham! Goodbye tuna, hello shark

Sharks are great killers. They swim well and have a good sense of smell. This helps them find their prey. Their large jaws have hundreds of sharp teeth.

Sharks eat tuna and a lot of other fish as well.

Could it kill me?

A shark could easily kill you with just one bite. It could take your leg off and let you bleed to death. There are more than 50 shark attacks on humans every year.

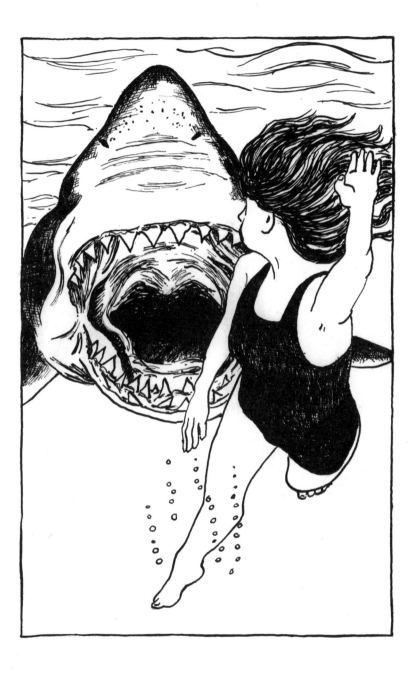

Wham! Goodbye shark, hello seabed

Only humans kill sharks, but those that are not hunted will die one day and float down to the seabed. The body rots and helps to feed the plants, so the story starts again.

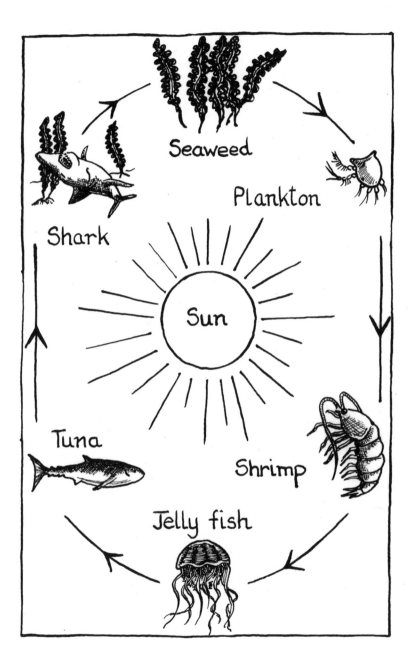

Wham! Fact file

The sea is blue because the colour of the sky reflects in it.

Female shrimps lay 50,000 to 1 million eggs at a time.

The mouth of a jelly fish is also where waste comes out.

Some tuna can swim as fast as 43mph (70kmh).

Sharks do not have any bones. Their skeleton is made of cartilage, which is softer than bone.

WHAM!

Also coming soon ...

Wham! Rainforest

Killer food chains in the hot rainforest!
Life in the rainforest is hard. Everything has to eat
– and everything gets eaten! From poison dart
frogs to jaguars, who comes out on top?